Rachmaninov

PIANO CONCERTO NO. 2, OP. 18
SOLO PIANO ARRANGEMENT

Sergei Vasil'evich Rachmaninov

Серге́й Васи́льевич Рахма́нинов

(1873~1943)

INDEX

Piano Concerto No.2

Solo Piano Arrangement

Arranged and Edited by
Isaac CHOI and Eun-han LEE

I

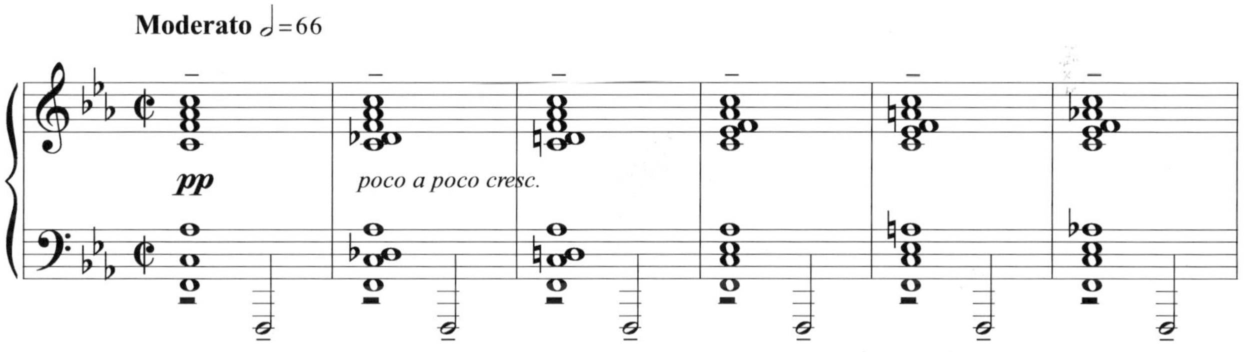

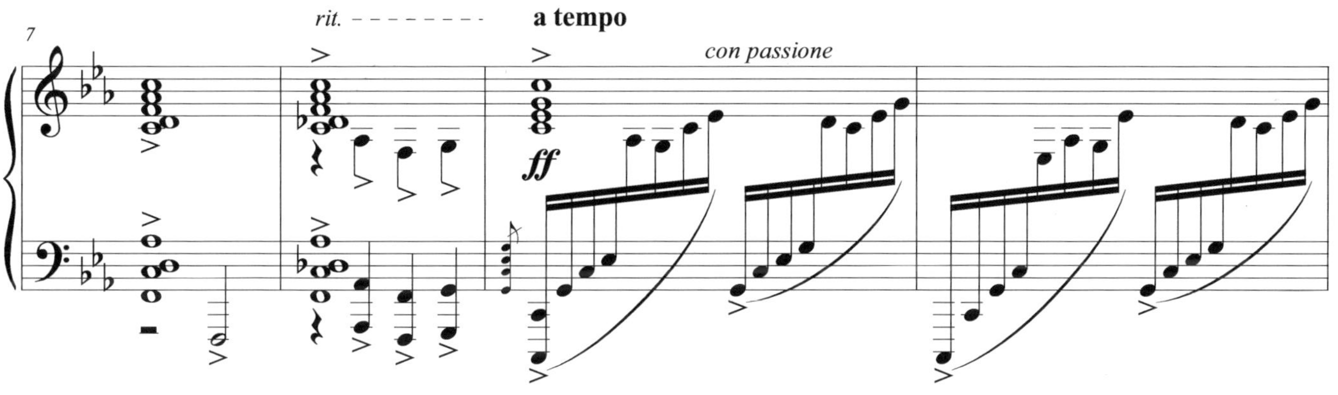

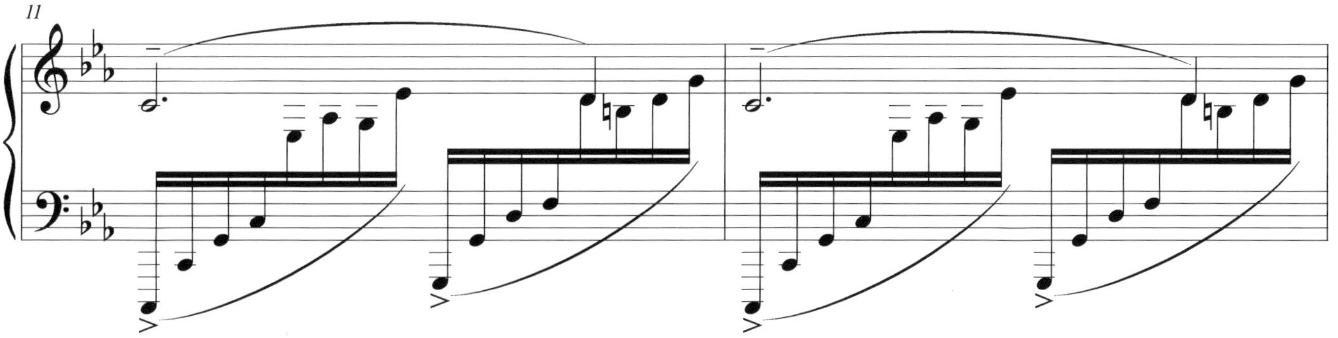

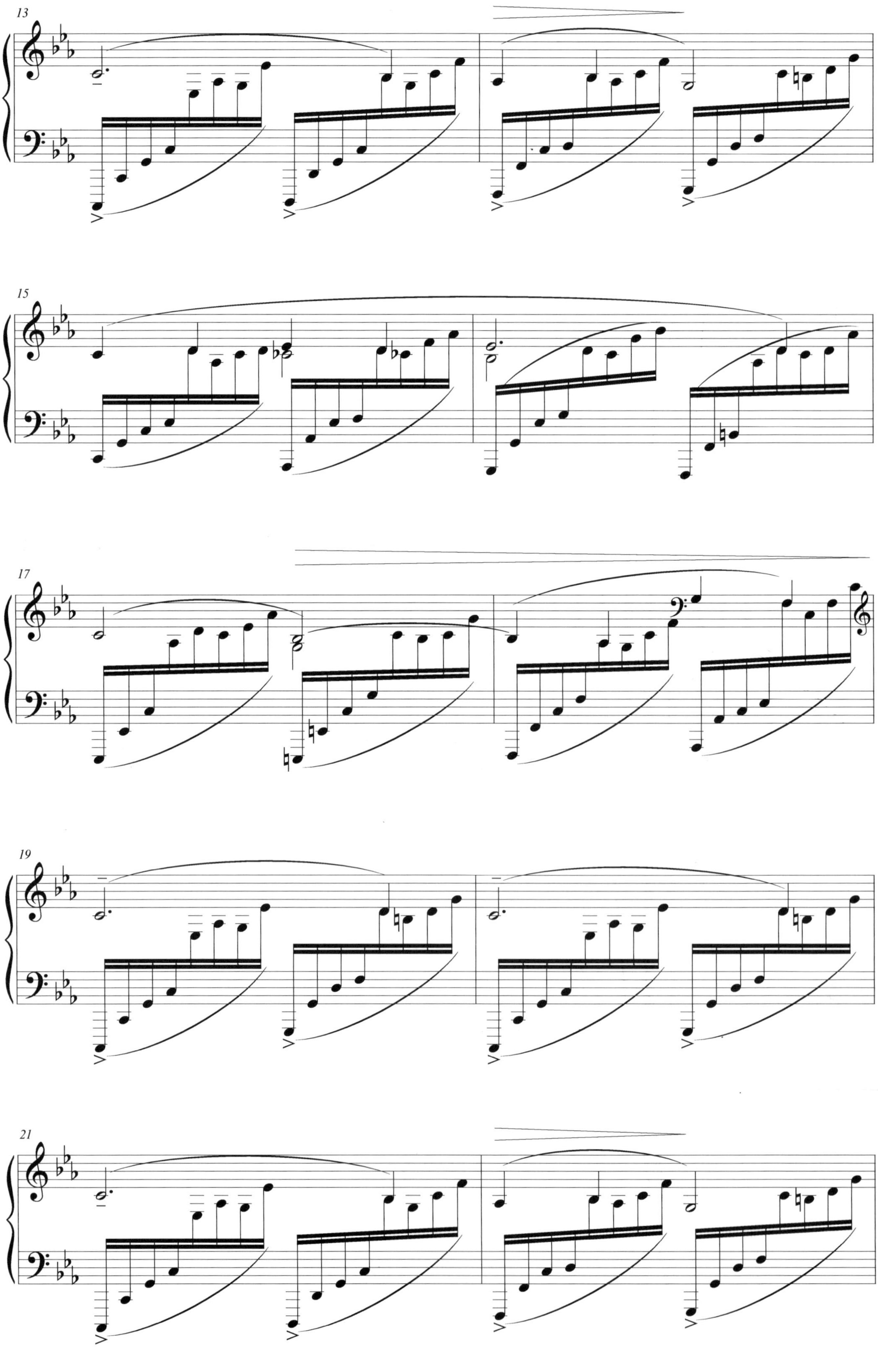
13
15
17
19
21

23
25
dim.
sempre marcato
p
mf
28
31
33

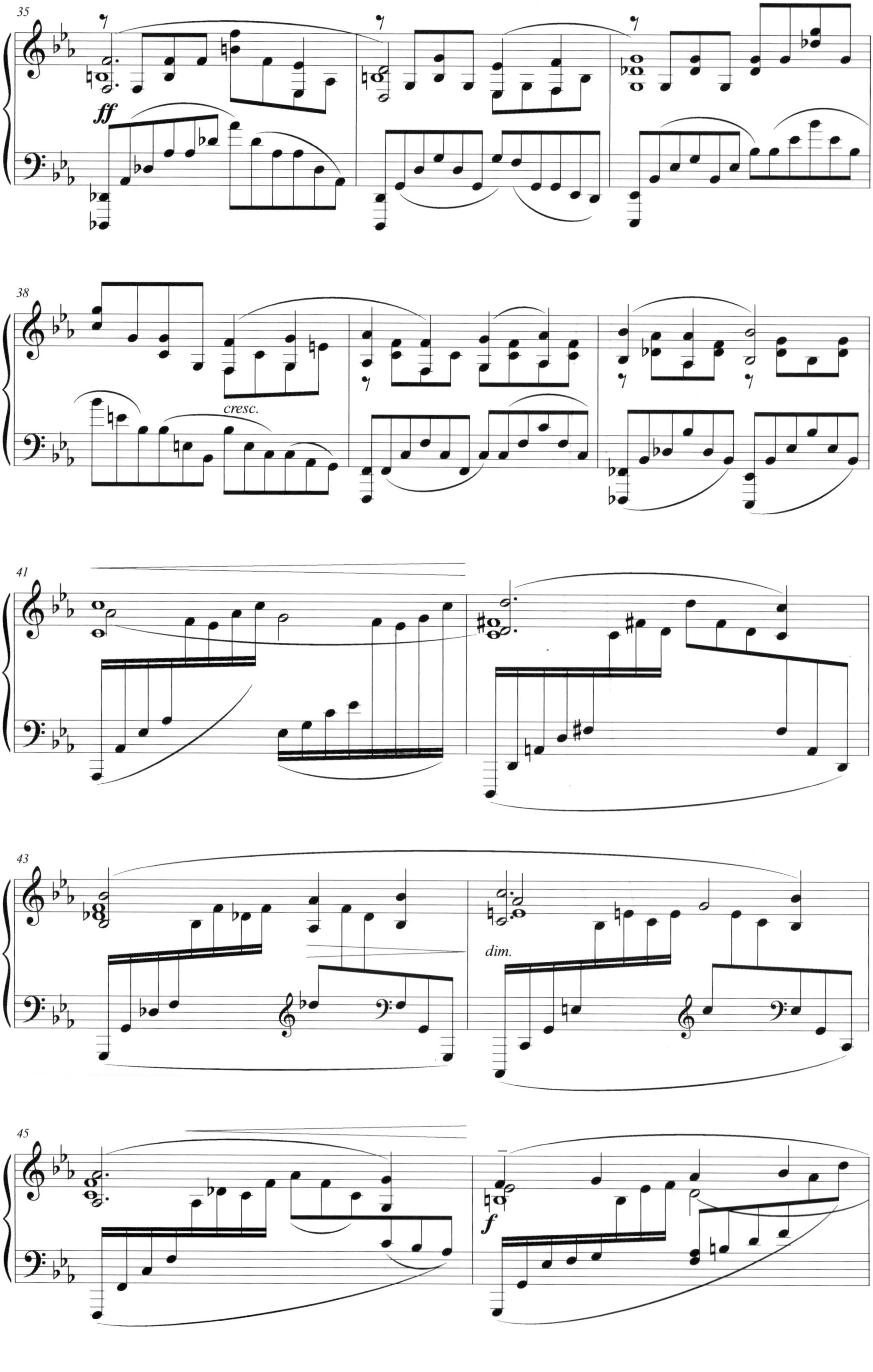
35
ff
38
cresc.
41
43
dim.
45
f

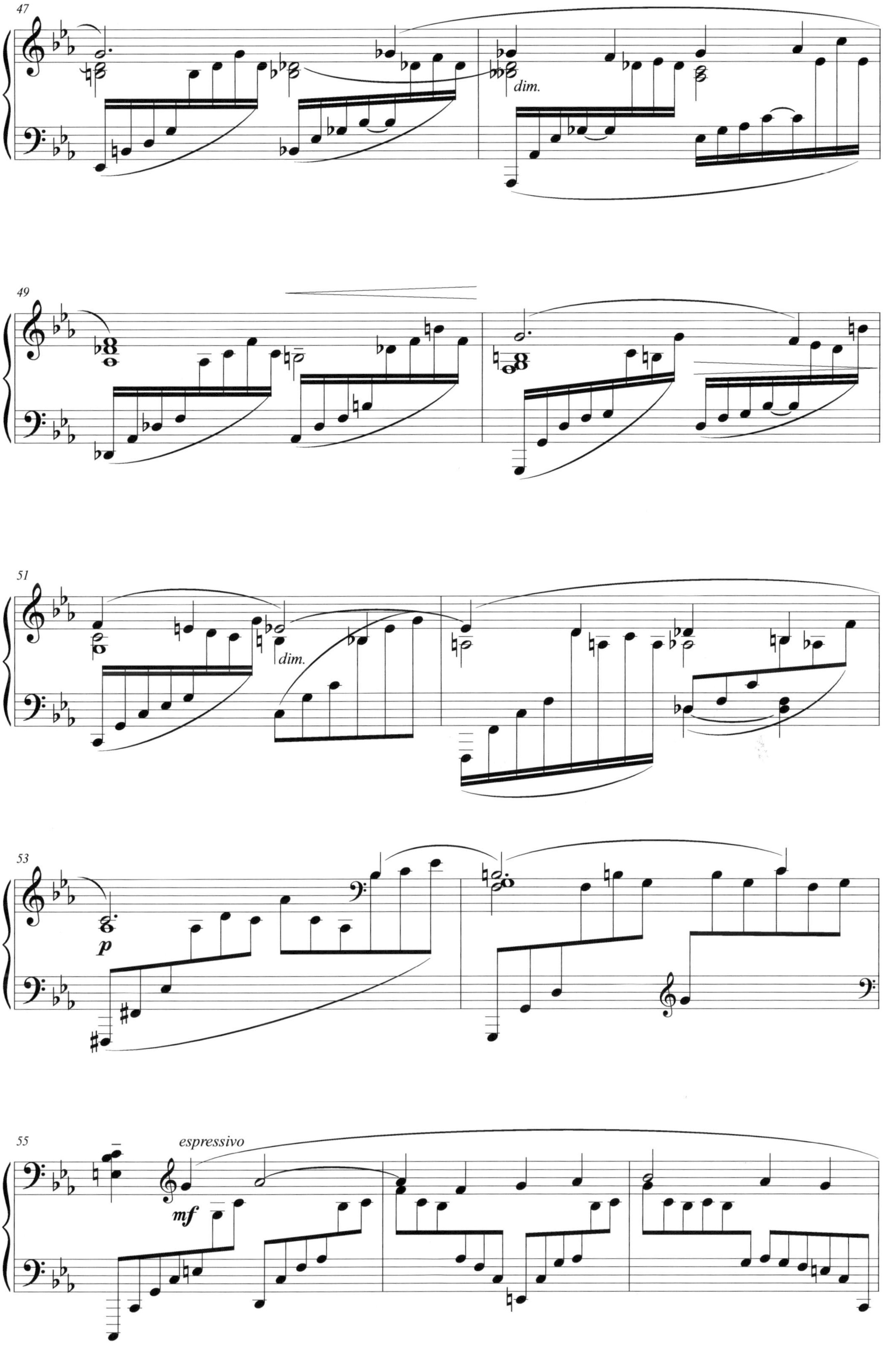
47
dim.
49
51
dim.
53
p
55
espressivo
mf

58
60
dim.
Un poco più mosso
63
pp
65
67

69
accel.
71
p
cresc.
76
cresc.
Tempo I
sff
pp
espressivo
mf
81
rit.
a tempo
m.d.
p
85

88
mf
92
rit.
a tempo
mf
96
99
rit.
mf
dim.
103
a tempo
p
cresc.

107
p
110
cresc.
f
112
dim.
f
114
116

118
120
mf
123
espressivo
p
126
m.g.
m.g.
130
m.g.
m.g.

8va
133
dolce
mf
6
6
dim.
(8va)
136
p
(8va)
139
Un poco più mosso (𝅗𝅥 = 72)
141
p
cresc.
8va
143

(8va)
145
f
dim.
147
149
151
pp
f pesante
p
154

156
dim.
158
pp
3
3
160
dim.
Moto precedente (𝅗𝅥 =72)
p
163
pp
167
p

171
pp
175
Più vivo (𝅗𝅥=76)
178
sf
p
181
pp
184

187
sf
190
cresc.
Più vivo (𝅗𝅥 = 80)
8va
193
sf
p
8va
195
8va
197
8va
p
8va

199
8va
201
8va
p
8va
203
8va
205
p
207
dim.

209
poco a poco acceler.
p
cresc.
f
212
cresc.
215
8va
f accel.
218
(8va)
221
(8va)

Allegro (𝅗𝅥=96)
(8va)
224
ff
228
8va
232
8va
(molto) rit.
3
3
(8va)
236
a tempo
marc.
f
p
cresc.
239

241
fff
rit.
243
Maestoso (Alla marcia)
245
ff
248
251
ff

254
257
rit.
Meno mosso (𝅗𝅥=76)
poco a poco cresc.
260
p
263
266

(poco a poco cresc.)
269
mf
272
275
ff
277
dim.
poco a poco calando
280
mf

282
284
mf
286
dim.
288
p
291
rit.

294
dim.
Moderato (𝅗𝅥=69)
296
pp
300
dim.
304
pp
308

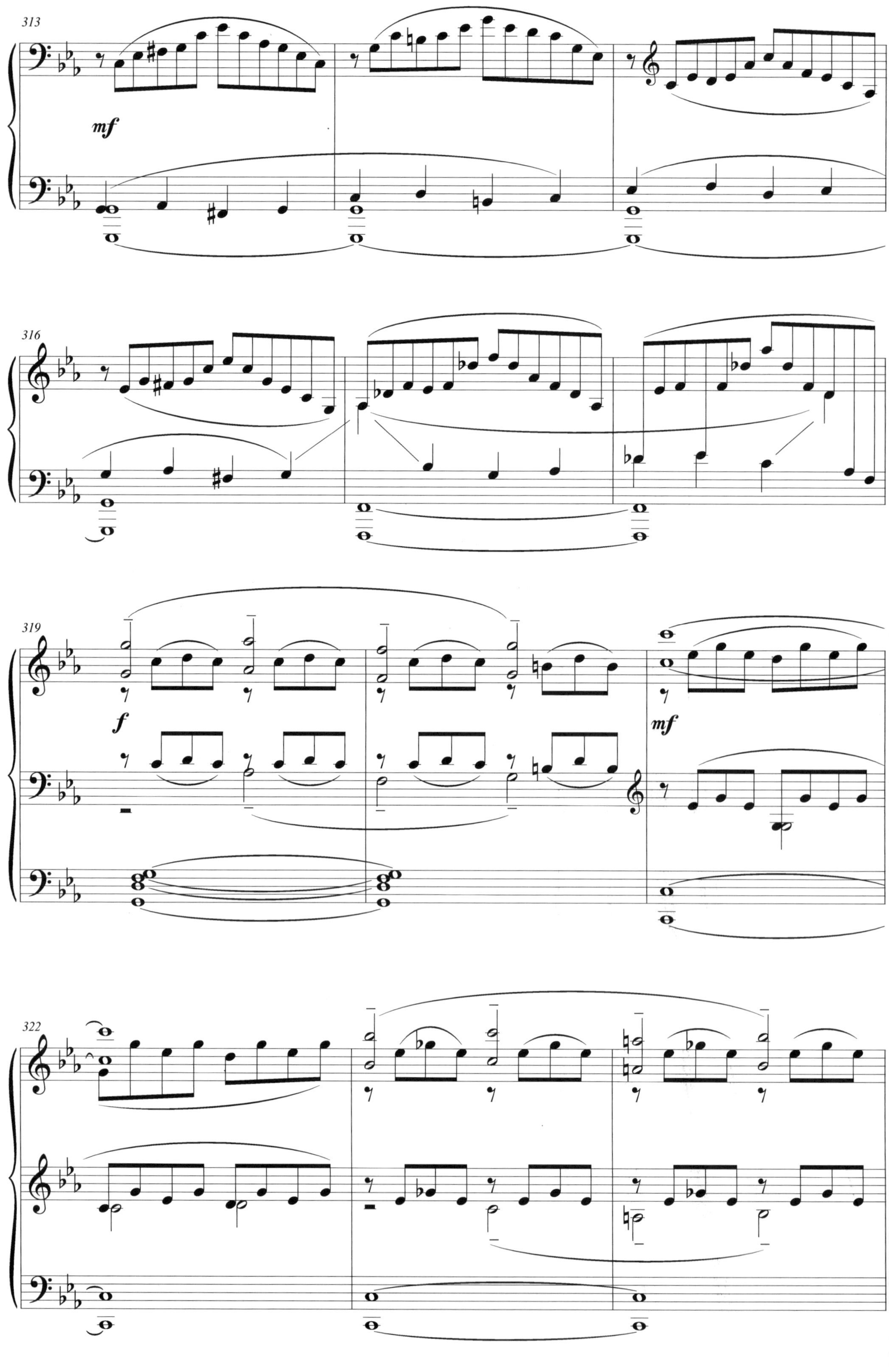
313
mf
316
319
f
mf
322

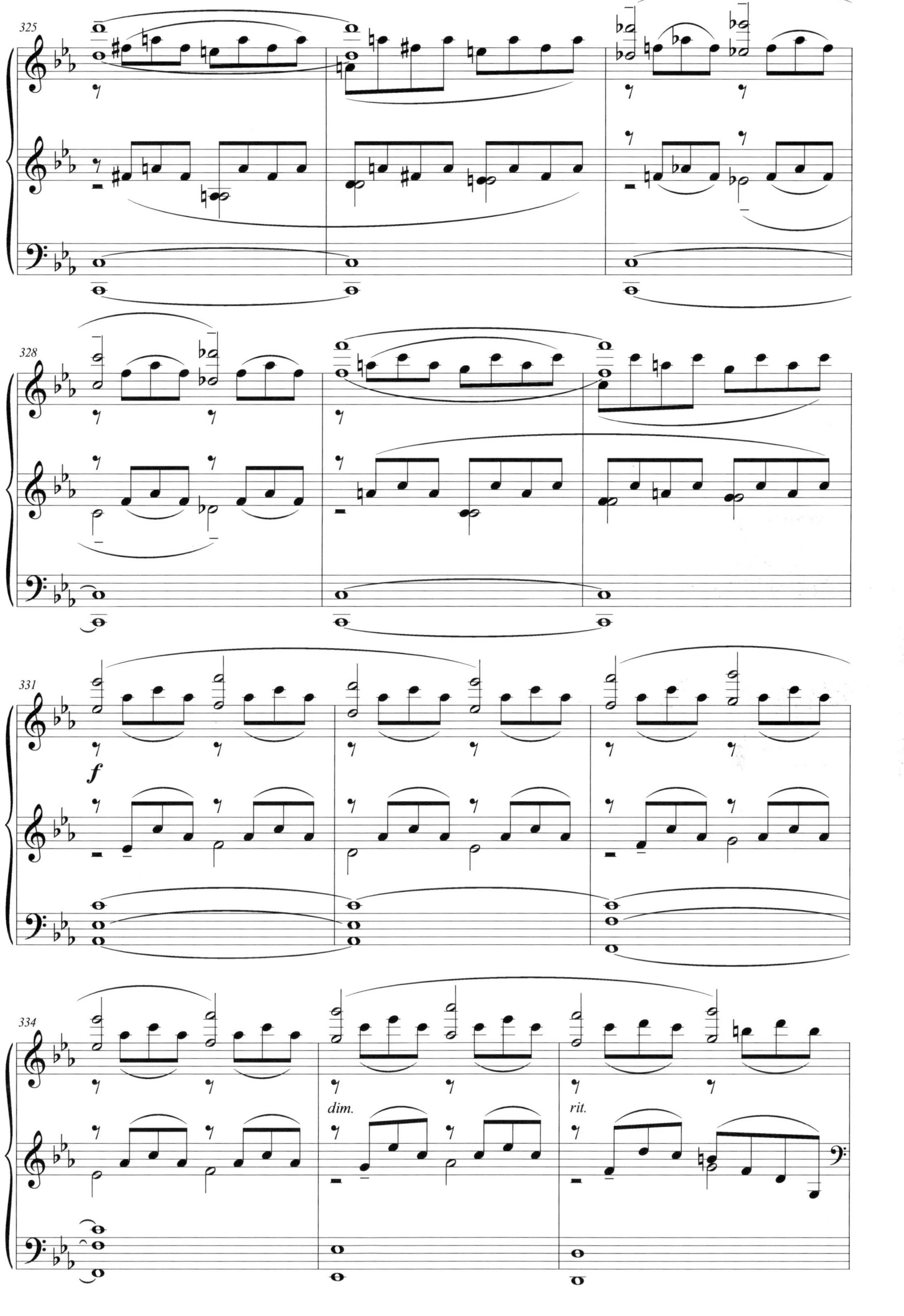
325
328
331
f
334
dim.
rit.

337
8va
pp
Un poco meno mosso
339
mf
341
mf
344
p
mf
347

350
dim.
Meno mosso (𝅗𝅥 = 63)
353
pp
355
m.g.
dim.
357
pp
359
p
m.g.
dim.

poco a poco acceler.
361
pp
363
pp
365
p
cresc.
368
f
p
cresc.
371
8va
sff
ff

II

Adagio sostenuto ♩ = 52

a tempo
m.g.
mf
p
f

23
rit.
dim.
a tempo
espressivo
mf
p
25
27
mf
29
mf
p

31
mf
33
mf
35
f
37
f
dim.

39
p
pp
42
(sempre legato)
45
m.d.
Un poco più animato
47
mf
50
p
mf

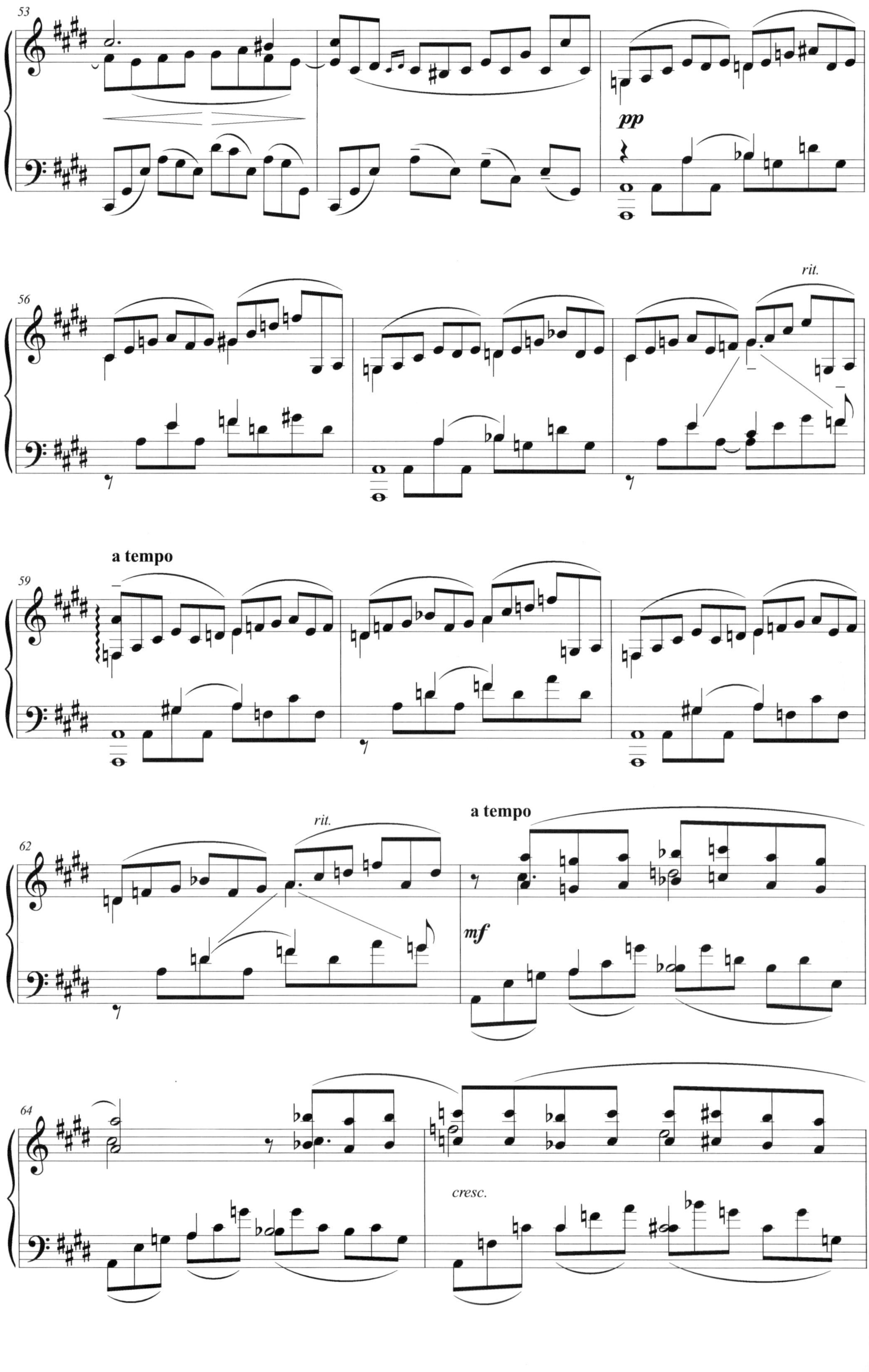
53
pp
56
rit.
a tempo
59
62
rit.
a tempo
mf
64
cresc.

allargando
66
ff
68
dim.
a tempo
mf
p
70
mf
72
p
75
mf

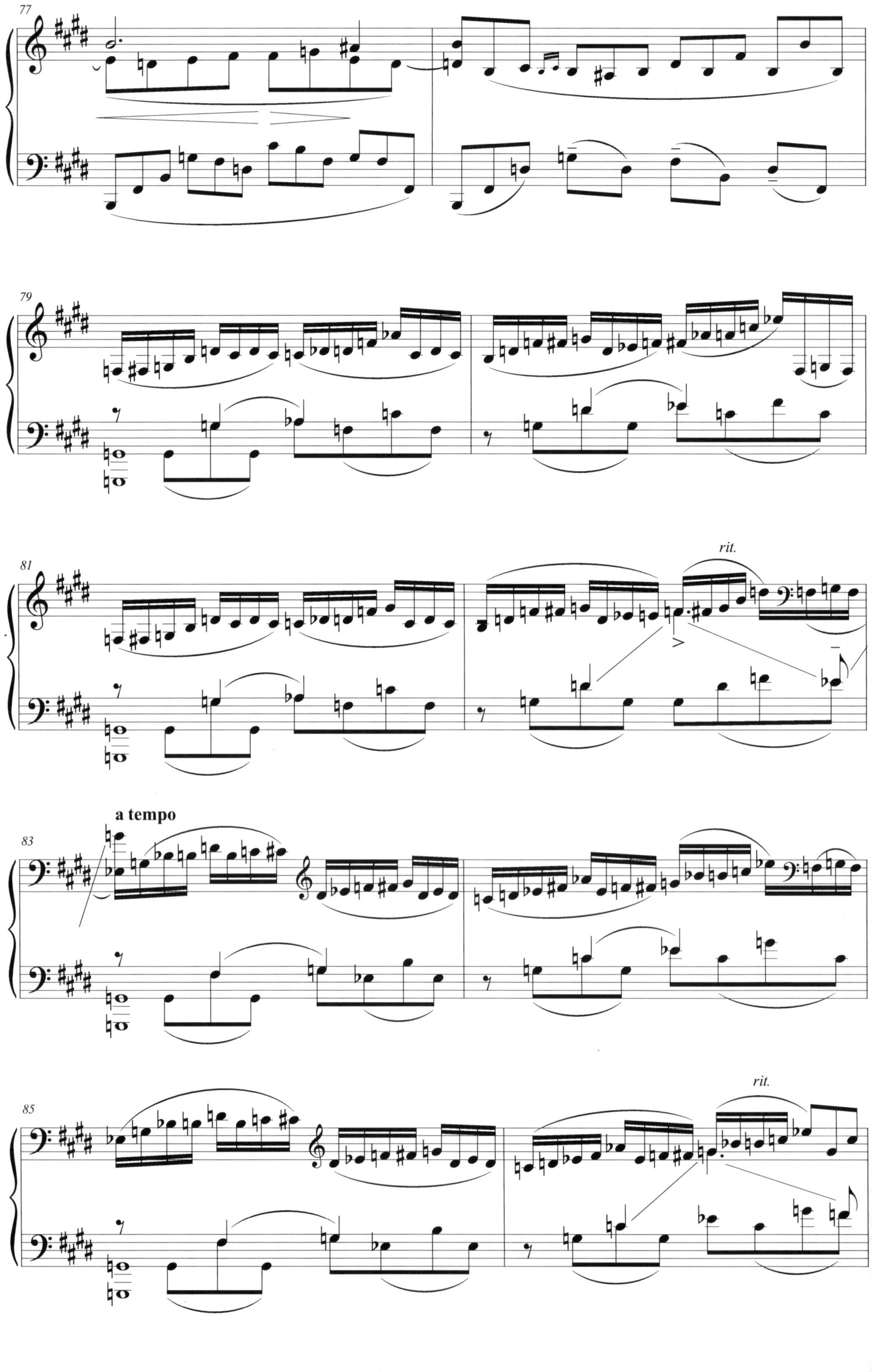
77
79
81
rit.
a tempo
83
85
rit.

a tempo
87
f
89
cresc.
allargando
91
ff
dim.
Più animato
93
p
95

97
p
99
101
p
cresc.
rit.
103
105
8va

106
(8va)
dim.
107
Più mosso
p
mf
sf
109
pp
110
ppp
mf
111
mf leggiero

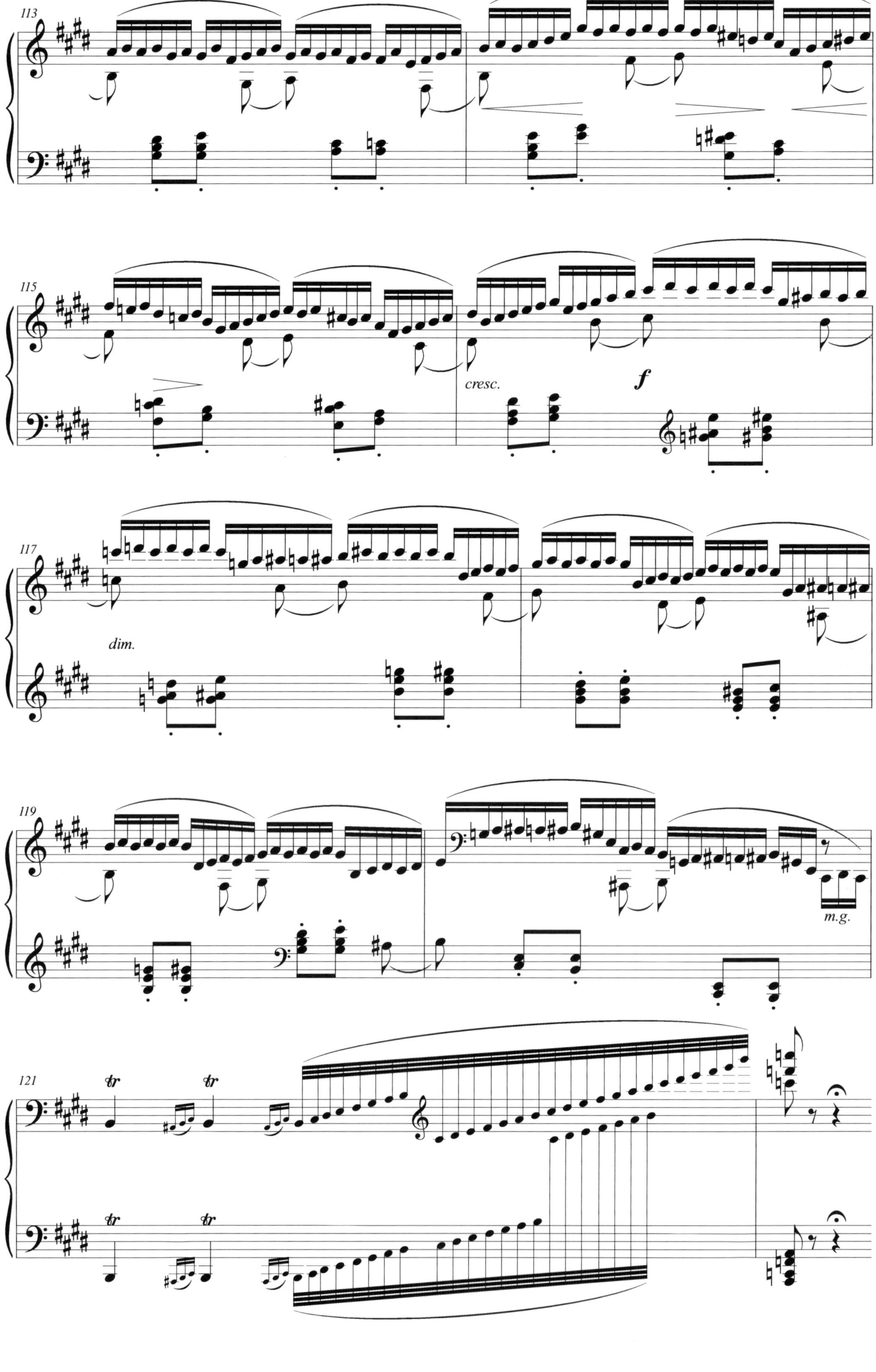
113
115
cresc.
f
117
dim.
119
m.g.
121
tr
tr
tr
tr

123
m.d.
125
8va
127
8va
ff
tr
m.d.
m.g.
p
128
p
mf
f
ff
8va
132
tr
f

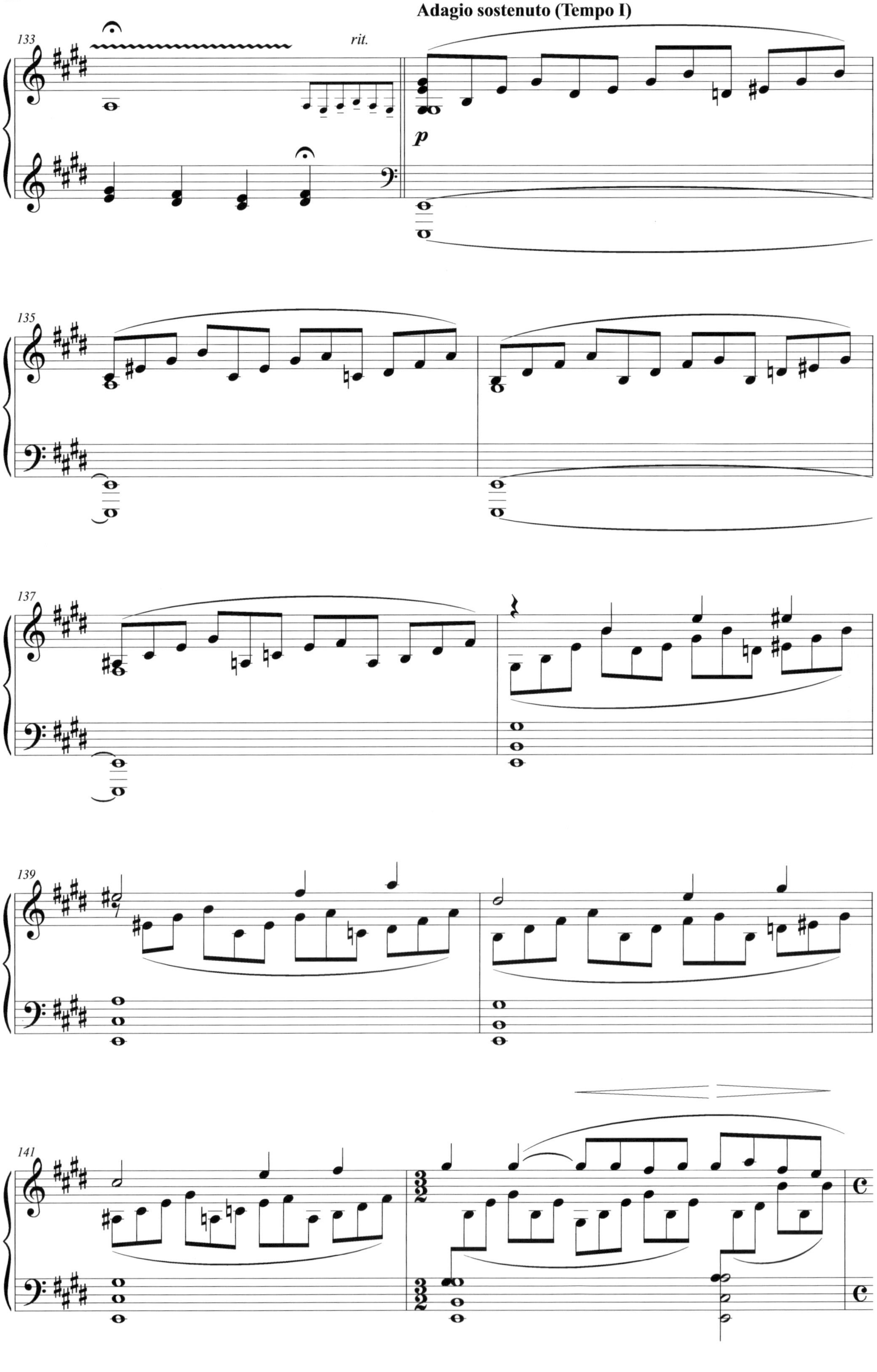
133
rit.
Adagio sostenuto (Tempo I)
p
135
137
139
141

143
mf
145
147
mf
p
149
151
f
dim.
rit.

a tempo
153
155
157
158
160

161
163
165
mf
p

III

Allegro scherzando 𝅗𝅥 = 116

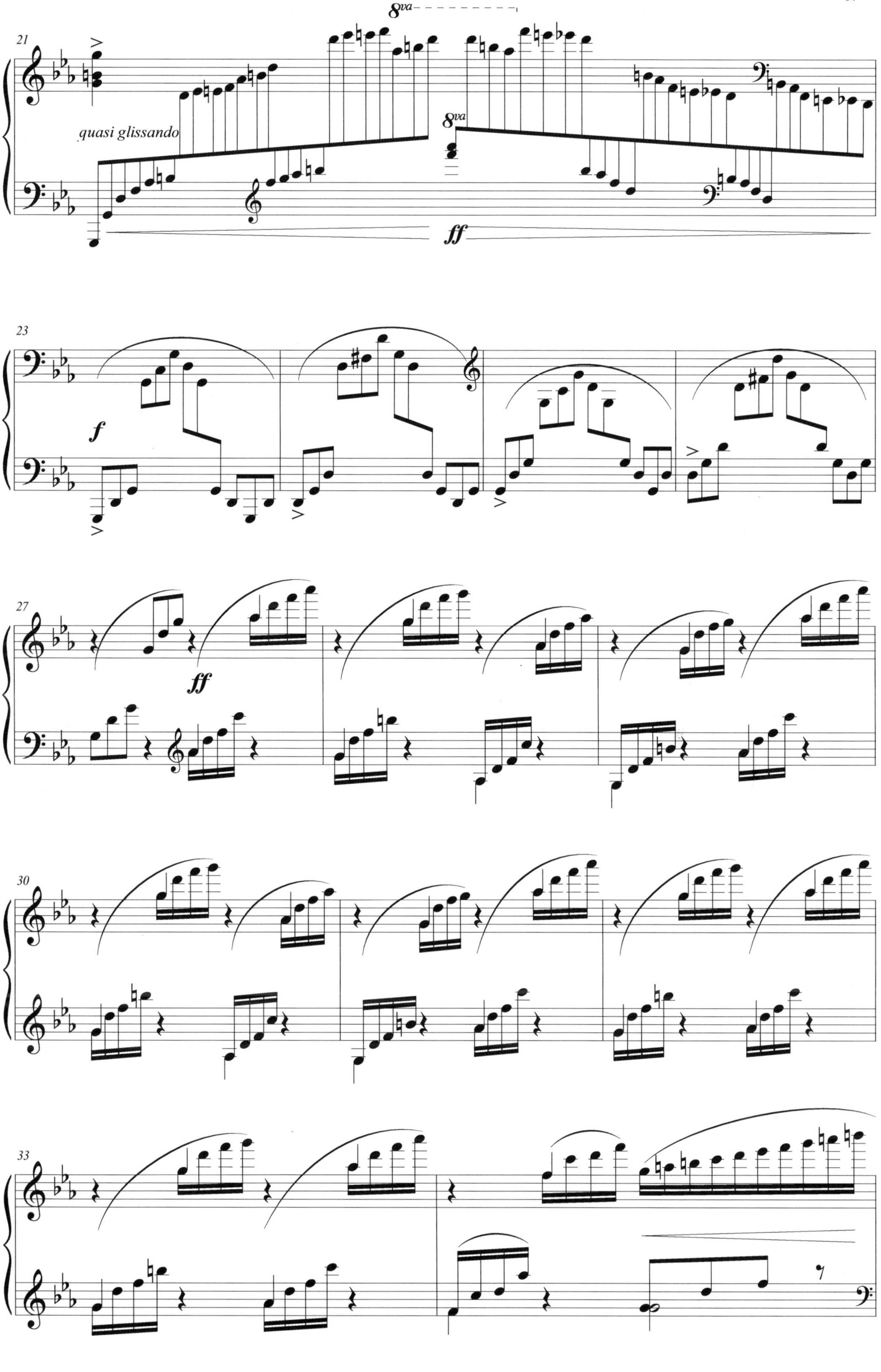
21
8va
quasi glissando
8va
ff
23
f
27
ff
30
33

35
sf
p
cresc.
39
f
dim.
p
f
43
mf
46
49
f
p

8va
52
pp
(8va)
55
(8va)
58
61
mf
63
3
3
f
mf
p

66
69
cresc.
72
8va
sf
(f)
p
75
mf
77
p

79
mf
81
p
83
86
cresc.
89
ff
m.d.
f

92
96
Meno mosso
f
100
dim.
104
Moderato (𝅗𝅥 = 72)
espress.
mf
108
m.d.

113
m.d.
m.g.
118
f
dim. e rit.
122
dolce
mf
126
130

134
f
138
f
142
cresc.
ff
146
mf
Meno mosso (𝅗𝅥 = 48)
149
rit.
legato

152
tr
155
tr
158
161
tr
Allegro scherzando (Moto primo) (𝅗𝅥 = 116)
p
cresc.
164
f
cresc.
ff
mf

167
ff
170
8va
8va
8va
8va
8va
fz
ff
174
(8va)
178
p
8va

Più mosso (𝅗𝅥 = 120)
180
(8va)
sf
8va
182
(8va)
f
184
p
8va
186
(8va)
accel.
f
Presto (𝅗𝅥 = 126)
188
8va
mf
ff
mf
8va
ff

192
(8va)
8va
8va
dim.
195
sf
sf
p
mf
p
mf
dim.
199
pp
205
mf
p
pp
p
pp
210
pp
p

215
p
220
mf
224
mf
dim.
228
p
pp
232
mf

236
pp
240
p staccato
244
cresc.
248
252
sf
dim.

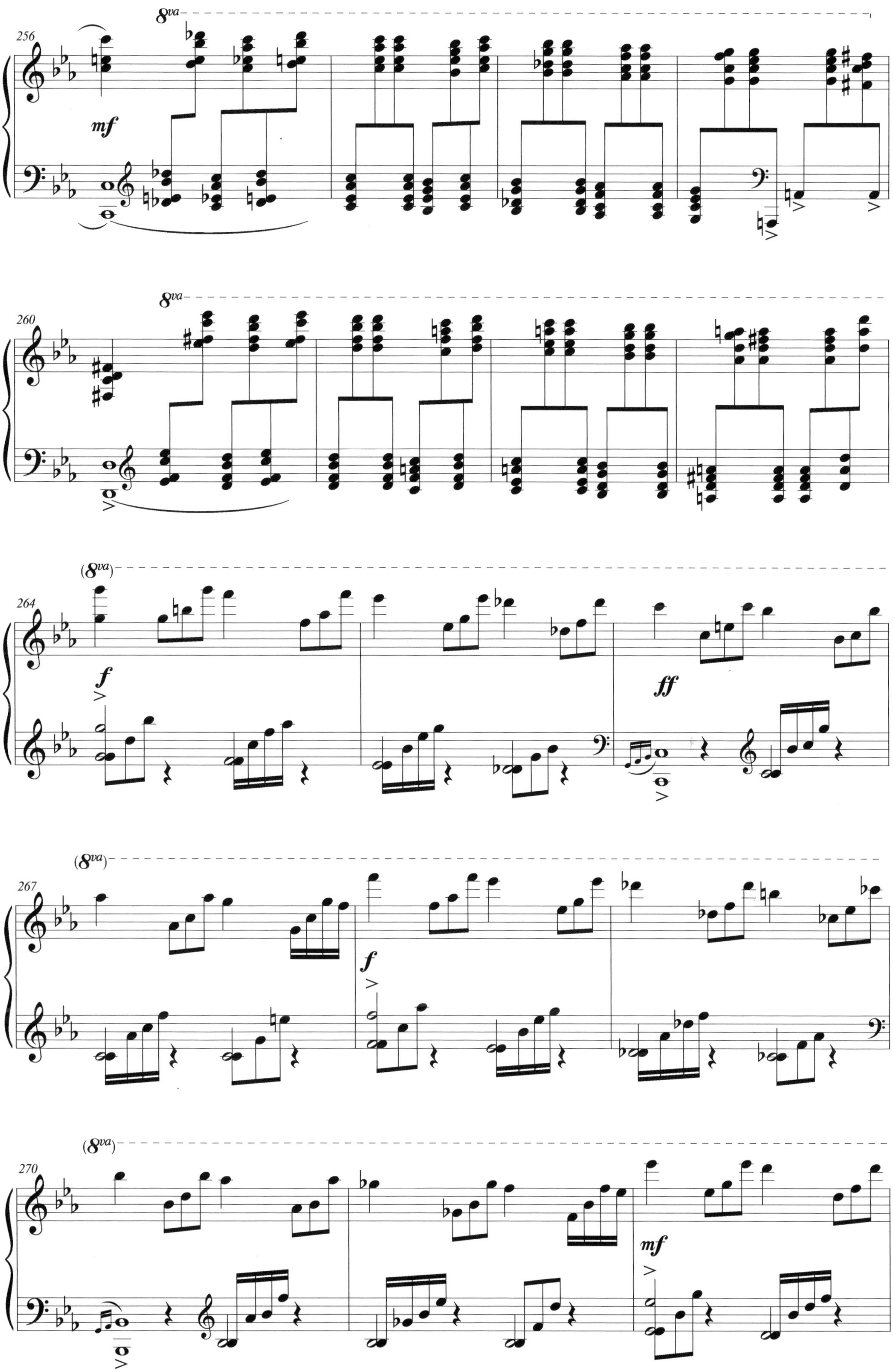
8va
256
mf
260
8va
264
(8va)
f
ff
267
(8va)
f
270
(8va)
mf

273
(8va)
276
280
mf
p
dim.
284
pp
8va
dim.
288
(8va)
ppp
cresc.
f

Più vivo (𝅗𝅥 = 132)
294
ff
298
Meno mosso (Come prima)
301
f
304
dim.
307
rit.

Moderato (𝅗𝅥=72)
310
mf
315
m.g.
320
325
329

333
337
340
8va
343
(8va)
346
cresc.

349
mf
352
rit.
Meno mosso (𝅗𝅥 = 48)
356
legato
358
361

364
(sopra)
(sotto)
(sopra)
366
Allegro scherzando (Moto primo) (𝅗𝅥 = ♩) (♩ = 116)
368
pp
p
371
374
p
mf

377
380
mf
cresc.
f
p
383
poco a poco accelerando
p
mf
385
387

389
3
3
391
8va
f
Alla breve
Agitato (𝅗𝅥 =76)
394
ff
p
3
396
398
cresc.

400
402
acceler.
405
408
cresc.
411

414
8va
(8va)
417
fff
(8va)
420
dim.
423
Presto (𝅗𝅥 = 132)
426
fff

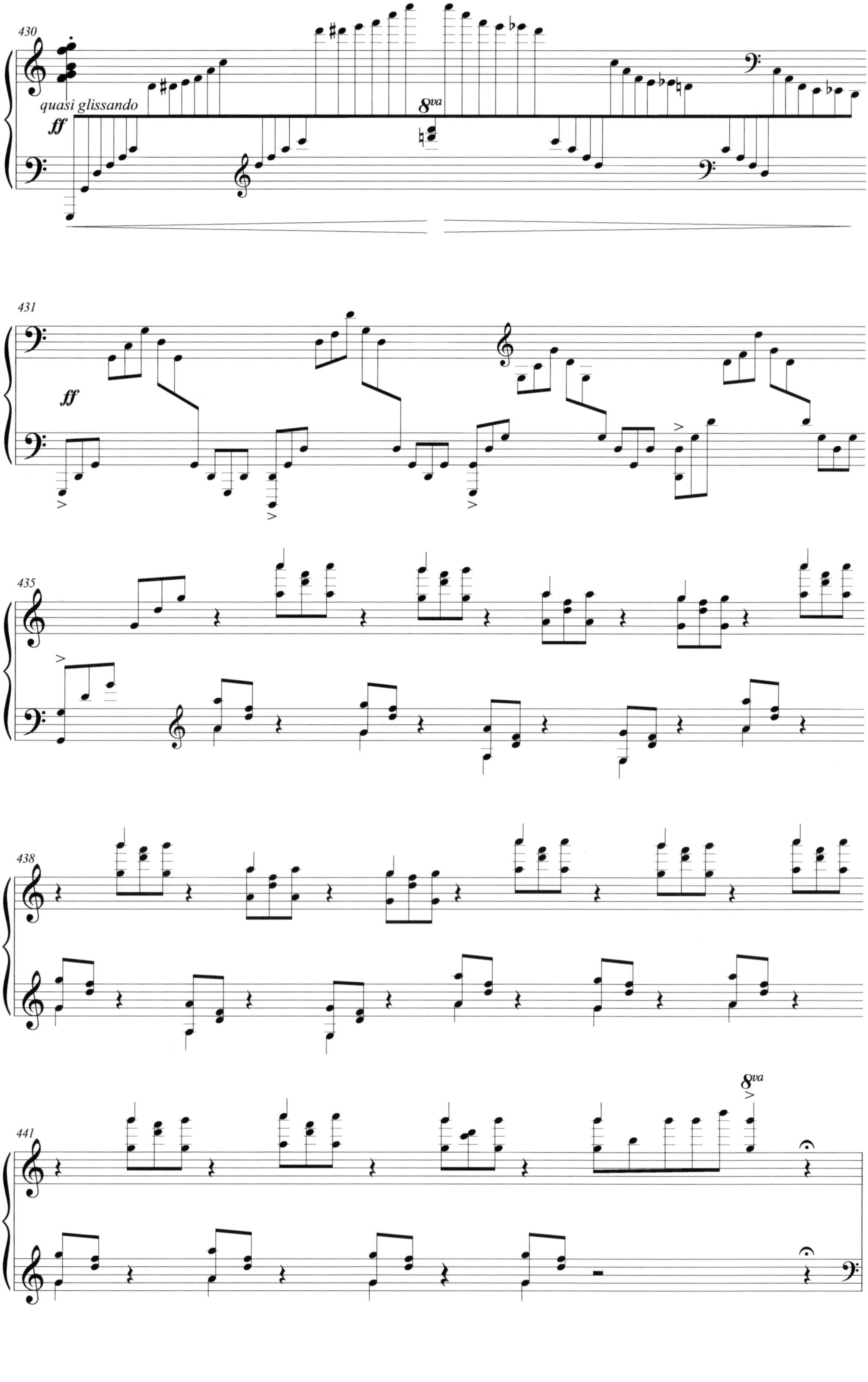
quasi glissando
ff
8va
ff
8va

Maestoso (𝅗𝅥 =60)
fff

Più vivo (𝅗𝅥 = 80)
ff
mf
Risoluto (𝅗𝅥 = 100)

8va
2
2
fff
(8va)
8va

RACHMANINOV

Piano Concerto No. 2, Op. 18

Solo piano arrangement

MUSICADDICTS EDITION

Composed by Sergei Rachmaninov

Arranged by MusicAddicts

Published by 엠에이기획

1st Printed in Feb. 14, 2017

출판사 엠에이기획

Tel. +82 32-343-0071

Facebook : @musicaddicts21

Price : 30 USD

ISBN : 9781520576435